James Herriot's
Yorkshire Revisited

James Herriot's
Yorkshire Revisited

Photographs by Derry Brabbs

Introduction by Jim Wight

ST. MARTIN'S PRESS
NEW YORK

LONDON

For extended copyright information see page 184.

ISBN 0-312-20629-1

First published in Great Britain by
Michael Joseph / the Penguin Group.

First U.S. Edition: November 1999

10 9 8 7 6 5 4 3 2 1

To James Herriot
who loved Yorkshire so much

Introduction by Jim Wight

One day, not long ago, I was standing on the close-cropped moorland grass beside the road which leads from Leyburn over Bellerby Moor to Grinton in Swaledale. I simply did as I had always done when coming to this particular spot; I gazed at the view with feelings of pleasure mixed with deep appreciation. I have stood here on many occasions, and familiarity with the surrounding scenery has done little to dampen the surge of excitement it generates in me.

Fifty-eight years previously, in 1940, my father Alfred Wight – better known to millions of his fans as the world bestselling author, James Herriot – stood for the very first time on this exact place. As a recently-qualified graduate of Glasgow Veterinary College, he had begun work in the Yorkshire market town of Thirsk, as assistant to Donald Sinclair. Donald had a partner in Leyburn, Frank Bingham – a charming but totally unambitious veterinary surgeon – who had little interest in making money out of tuberculin testing the countless numbers of cattle that frequented his part of Yorkshire. That job fell to the young James Herriot, and his journeys across to the Yorkshire Dales was his introduction to a part of the world that thrilled him from that very first day, many years ago on Bellerby Moor.

It can be disappointing to revisit places that hold sweet memories: they become imprinted upon the mind, radiating an image that remains unaltered as the years skim by. Unfortunately, the march of progress and the influence of an ever-changing world often results in our remembering a vastly different picture of our favourite places – and it can be a salutory and depressing experience when one is let down.

I have occasionally felt sadness and disappointment on returning to some of my boyhood haunts, but my feelings as I stood that day on the windswept moor above Swaledale were, happily, very different – ones not only of nostalgia but of gratitude. I realised that James Herriot's favourite Yorkshire Dales – Swaledale, Wensleydale and Coverdale – have hardly changed. The scene laid out before me was virtually the same one that had entranced my father all those years ago.

James Herriot's books captured the imagination of countless people, and many, including the author himself, have attempted to analyse the real reasons behind his success. In 1974, in an address to the Harrogate Medical Society, he said: 'I think that people like my stories because they are reaching out for the simple things which they, in their materialistic and urbanised society, have lost – old, unspoiled Yorkshire and a way of life so different from their own.'

This is probably true but it does not tell the whole story. In the early years of his success, I read his books as he wanted them to be read – purely for enjoyment. I appreciated them mainly for their humour; they were very funny and the rich characterisation of such unforgettable characters as Siegfried and Tristan added greatly to the effect. But there was something more. There was a quality in the writing that lifted James Herriot's work above the level of the ordinary story-teller: his wonderful powers of description. Through the use of well-chosen words, the author's genuine love of the countryside in which he spent his life not only infected his readers with that enthusiasm, it swept them right into his world. His passion for Yorkshire is now shared by millions.

This magnificently illustrated book concenrates on that aspect of James Herriot's writing, and the text accompanying Derry Brabbs's beautiful photographs clearly portrays the feeling my father felt for his surroundings.

Alfred Wight had felt a burning desire to write a book from his very earliest days as a veterinary surgeon. He had always been a great reader with an admiration of the descriptive powers displayed by such classical authors as Dickens and Sir Walter Scott. This stood him in good stead in his future years as a writer. As his veterinary career progressed, the desire to write a book intensified. He wanted to write about the unique farming characters with their strange remedies for their ailing stock; he wished to describe the old Yorkshire that fascinated him from the day he first set foot in it; but, above all, he wanted to preserve in print a way of life that was being blown away on the winds of change that were sweeping across his profession.

All this, of course, he achieved, and it is the vivid and heartfelt descriptions of the backcloth to that life that is largely responsible for his incredible success, and this can be fully felt within the pages of this book.

His most successful book was *James Herriot's Yorkshire*, first published twenty years ago in 1979. That book, also illustrated with Derry Brabbs's photographs, resulted in a tourist explosion as millions of fans invaded Yorkshire to see the famous vet's favourite places for themselves.

On the cover of the book there is a picture of my father standing with his black labrador, Dan, on the top of the Hambleton Hills, looking westwards towards the Pennines; *see* the illustration on page 5. This is a wonderfully apt cover for such a book since, from that very spot, a vast area of North Yorkshire can be seen – an area now known, thanks to the massive success of his books, as 'Herriot Country'.

On opening the book, it is the wild moors and green valleys of the Yorkshire Dales that seem to receive the most attention, matching that captivating area of Yorkshire that provides the background for his stories, despite the famous Yorkshire vet having spent almost his entire working life in the country around Thirsk, some twenty-five to the east.

When Alfred Wight first came to Yorkshire he received a surprise. He had always considered it to be a dull and rather stodgy county, but his first sight of Thirsk, followed by a trip into the Hambleton Hills and the North York Moors, were a revelation. He said to me many time that he considered himself to be a very fortunate man to have spent his working life in such wonderful countryside — words that are echoed in his second book: 'Probably it was because I hadn't dreamed there was a place like the Dales. I hadn't thought it possible that I could spend all my days in a high, clean-blown land where the scent of grass or trees was never far away; and where even in the driving rain of winter I could snuff the air and find the freshness of growing things hidden somewhere in the cold clasp of winter. My work consisted now of driving from farm to farm across the roof of England with a growing conviction that I was a privileged person.'

The Yorkshire Dales however had an extra quality — a touch of magic that never failed to excite him. The photograph on the cover of James Herriot's Yorkshire says it all. He is standing on top of Sutton Bank east of Thirsk, one of his very favourite places, but his face is turned westwards to a part of Yorkshire that meant just that little bit more.

When my father was writing his first book, he wanted to remain as anonymous as possible. For this reason, he decided to set his stories in the Dales rather than around Thirsk which was where the vast majority had their origins. Thirsk was in his

mind as he described Darrowby, but the limestone country of the Dales, with the stone walls snaking down from the high fells, was forever in front of his eyes. This has resulted in the Yorkshire Dales having pride of place whenever 'Herriot Country' is mentioned and, indeeed, it is so in this book although the purple North York Moors are also well represented. My father was very secretive about the real places he was describing in his stories and very few people knew the specific locations; for this reason, no captions have been included in the book. The photographs have been chosen as being evocative of my father's prose.

One reason for my father visiting the Yorkshire Dales so often throughout his life was that it was there that he found peace and tranquillity. He wrote in his second book: 'As I drove west across the Plain of York I began to catch glimpses over the hedge tops of the long spine of the Pennines lifting into the morning sky, and when the hedges gave way to the clean limestone walls I had the feeling I always had of the world opening out, of shackles falling away.'

In his very early years in Thirsk, he travelled regularly into the Dales to help Frank Bingham, who soon became a very firm friend, and some of the memories were hard ones – long, lonely miles over moorland roads, often in appalling weather and in incredibly spartan little cars. In the years following the 1940s, however, the Dales ceased to be his working arena; instead they became a place of recreation and happy memories. Perhaps this is one reason he writes about them with such affection.

In 1978 he bought a cottage in Coverdale and visited it at all times of year and in all weathers. Some of the local people, ones who endured a hard life attempting to eke a living from their wild surroundings, could not understand his attraction for the place. They knew he was a famous man who could, should he so wish, have spent his holidays on sun-drenched beaches in exotic parts of the world.

One dark and stormy October day, a farmer from the village approached him and asked him why he had chosen such a bleak spot. The answer is simple. My father loved the Dales in all their moods and never tired of revisiting them. In the last year of his life, when he was so ill, I would drive him into the Dales and he would sit quietly for hours, taking in the scenery around him that must have stirred so many happy memories.

James Herriot was a man who never failed to appreciate the beauty of his surroundings and this quality is vividly illustrated in the many extracts of his writing that appear in this book. Many have journeyed to savour his favourite corners of Yorkshire; to leaf through these pages will enable readers to do so without even moving from the comfort of their armchair. James Herriot's books can be read many times over, each occasion with as much enjoyment as the last. Just as his favourite part of the world – unspoiled Yorkshire – will be revisited for many years to come.

It was hot in the rickety little bus and I was on the wrong side where the July sun beat on the windows. I shifted uncomfortably inside my best suit and eased a finger inside the constricting white collar. It was a foolish outfit for this weather but a few miles ahead my prospective employer was waiting for me and I had to make a good impression.

We had been climbing steadily now for the last fifteen miles or so, moving closer to the distant blue swell of the Pennines. I had never been in Yorkshire before but the name had always raised a picture of a county as stodgy and unromantic as its pudding; I was prepared for solid worth, dullness and a total lack of charm. But as the bus groaned its way higher I began to wonder. The formless heights were resolving into high, grassy hills and wide valleys. In the valley bottoms, rivers twisted among the trees and solid greystone farmhouses lay among islands of cultivated land which pushed bright green promontories up the hillsides into the dark tide of heather which lapped from the summits.

I saw the fences and hedges give way to dry stone walls which bordered the roads, enclosed the fields and climbed endlessly over the surrounding fells. The walls were everywhere, countless miles of them, tracing their patterns high on the green uplands.

Darrowby didn't get much space in the guide books but when it was mentioned it was described as a grey little town on the river Darrow with a cobbled market place and little of interest except its two ancient bridges. But when you looked at it, its setting was beautiful on the pebbly river where the houses clustered thickly and straggled unevenly along the lower slopes of Herne Fell. Everywhere in Darrowby, in the streets, through the windows of the houses you could see the Fell rearing its calm, green bulk more than two thousand feet above the huddled roofs.

I got out and stood beside my battered suitcase, looking about me. There was something unusual and I couldn't put my finger on it at first. Then I realised what it was – the silence. The other passengers had dispersed, the driver had switched off his engine and there was not a sound or a movement anywhere. The only visible sign of life was a group of old men sitting round the clock tower in the centre of the square but they might have been carved from stone.

Once clear of the market place, the road dipped quite suddenly and we could see all of the Dale stretching away from us in the evening sunshine. The outlines of the great hills were softened in the gentle light and a broken streak of silver showed where the Darrow wandered on the valley floor.

We'll go home a different way.' Farnon leaned over the driving wheel and wiped the cracked windscreen with his sleeve. 'Over the Brenkstone Pass and down Sildale. It's not much further and I'd like you to see it.'

We took a steep, winding road, climbing higher and still higher with the hillside falling away sheer to a dark ravine where a rocky stream rushed headlong to the gentler country below. On the top, we got out of the car. In the summer dusk, a wild panorama of tumbling fells and peaks rolled away and lost itself in the crimson and gold ribbons of the western sky. To the east, a black mountain overhung us, menacing in its naked bulk. Huge, square-cut boulders littered the lower slopes.

I whistled softly as I looked around. This was different from the friendly hill country I had seen on the approach to Darrowby.

Farnon turned towards me. 'Yes, one of the wildest spots in England. A fearsome place in winter. I've know this pass to be blocked for weeks on end.'

I pulled the clean air deeply into my lungs. Nothing stirred in the vastness, but a curlew cried faintly and I could just hear the distant roar of the torrent a thousand feet below.

It was dark when we got into the car and started the long descent into Sildale. The valley was a shapeless blur but points of light showed where the lonely farms clung to the hillsides.

With the passage of time, an appreciation of the Dales people had grown in me; a sense of the value of their carefully given friendship. The higher up the country, the more I liked them. At the bottom of the valley, where it widened into the plain, the farmers were like farmers everywhere, but the people grew more interesting as the land heightened, and in the scattered hamlets and isolated farms near the bleak tops I found their characteristics most marked; their simplicity and dignity, their rugged independence and their hospitality.

This Sunday morning it was the Bellerbys and they lived at the top of Halden, a little valley branching off the main Dale. My car bumped and rattled over the last rough mile of an earth road with the tops of boulders sticking up every few yards.

I got out and from where I stood, high at the head, I could see all of the strangely formed cleft in the hills, its steep sides grooved and furrowed by countless streams feeding the boisterous Halden Beck which tumbled over its rocky bed far below. Down there were trees and some cultivated fields, but immediately behind me the wild country came crowding in on the bowl where the farmhouse lay. Halsten Pike, Alstang, Birnside – the huge fells with their barbarous names were very near.

I hardly noticed the passage of the weeks as I rattled along the moorland roads on my daily rounds; but the district was beginning to take shape, the people to emerge as separate personalities. Most days I had a puncture. The tyres were through to the canvas on all wheels; it surprised me that they took me anywhere at all.

But it was a fine summer and long days in the open gave me a tan which rivalled the farmers'. Even mending a puncture was no penance on the high, unfenced roads with the wheeling curlews for company and the wind bringing the scents of flowers and trees up from the valleys. And I could find other excuses to get out and sit on the crisp grass and look out over the airy roof of Yorkshire. It was like taking time out of life. Time to get things into perspective and assess my progress. Everything was so different that it confused me. This countryside after years of city streets, the sense of release from exams and study, the job with its daily challenge.

I looked again at the slip of paper where I had written my visits. 'Dean, 3, Thompson's Yard. Old dog ill.'

There were a lot of these 'yards' in Darrowby. They were, in fact, tiny streets, like pictures from a Dickens novel. Some of them opened off the market place and many more were scattered behind the main thoroughfares in the old part of the town. From the outside you could see only an archway and it was always a surprise to me to go down a narrow passage and come suddenly upon the uneven rows of little houses with no two alike, looking into each other's windows across eight feet of cobbles.

We went through the door into the long garden. I had found that even the lowliest dwellings in Darrowby had long strips of land at the back as though the builders had taken it for granted that the country people who were going to live in them would want to occupy themselves with the pursuits of the soil; with vegetable and fruit growing, even stock keeping in a small way. You usually found a pig there, a few hens, often pretty beds of flowers.

That evening, Tristan came out with me on my last visit. The case was simple enough – a cow with an infected eye – but the farm was in a village high up the Dale, and when we finished, it was dusk. I felt good, and everything seemed to stand out, clear and meaningful. The single, empty, grey stone street, the last red streaks in the sky, the dark purple of the enclosing fells. There was no wind, but a soft breath came from the quiet moors, sweet and fresh and full of promise. Among the houses, the thrilling smell of wood smoke was everywhere.

It was dark when I left the farm. About five o'clock on a late December day, the light gone early and the stars beginning to show in a frosty sky. I was within half a mile of Darrowby with the lights of the little town beginning to wink between the bare roadside branches.

It was difficult at first to shake off the mantle of unreality in which I had wrapped myself last night. Last night – Christmas Eve. It had been like a culmination of all the ideas I had ever held about Christmas – a flowering of emotions I had never experienced before. It had been growing in me since the call to a tiny village where the snow lay deep on the single street and on the walls and on the ledges of the windows; and as I left it I drove beneath the laden branches of a group of dark spruce as motionless as though they had been sketched against the white background of the fields. People, anonymously muffled, were hurrying about, doing their last-minute shopping, their feet slithering over the rounded stones.

Before going to bed and just as the church bells began I closed the door of Skeldale House behind me and walked again into the market place. Nothing stirred now in the white square stretching smooth and cold and empty under the moon, and there was a Dickens look about the ring of houses and shops put together long before anybody thought of town planning; tall and short, fat and thin, squashed in crazily around the cobbles, their snow-burdened roofs jagged and uneven against the frosty sky.

As I walked back, the snow crunching under my feet, the bells clanging, the sharp air tingling in my nostrils, the wonder and mystery of Christmas enveloped me in a great wave. Peace on earth, goodwill towards men; the words became meaningful as never before and I saw myself suddenly as a tiny particle in the scheme of things; Darrowby, the farmers, the animals and me seemed for the first time like a warm, comfortable entity. I hadn't been drinking but I almost floated up the stairs to bed.

Beyond the village the road climbed steeply then curved around the rim of the valley in a wide arc. I always slowed down here and there was always something different to see, but today the vast chequerboard of fields and farms and woods stood out with a clarity I had never seen before. The distance was magically fore-shortened in the clear, frosty air and I felt I could reach out and touch the familiar landmarks far below.

I looked back at the enormous white billows and folds of the fells, crowding close, one upon another into the blue distance, every crevice uncannily defined, the highest summits glittering where the sun touched them. I could see the village with the Kirbys' cottage at the end. I had found Christmas and peace and goodwill and everything back there.

Farmers? They were the salt of the earth.

I realised, quite suddenly, that spring had come. It was late March and I had been examining some sheep in a hillside fold. On my way down, in the lee of a small pine wood I leaned my back against a tree and was aware, all at once, of the sunshine, warm on my closed eyelids, the clamour of the larks, the muted sea-sound of the wind in the high branches. And though the snow still lay in long runnels behind the walls and the grass was lifeless and winter-yellowed, there was the feeling of change; almost of liberation, because, unknowing, I had surrounded myself with a carapace against the iron months, the relentless cold.

It wasn't a warm spring but it was dry with sharp winds which fluttered the white heads of the snowdrops and bent the clumps of daffodils on the village greens. In April the roadside banks were bright with the fresh yellow of the primroses.

And the lambs. All young animals are appealing but the lamb has been given an unfair share of charm. The moments come back: of a bitterly cold evening when I had delivered twins on a wind-scoured hillside; the tiny lambs shaking their heads convulsively and within minutes one of them struggling upright and making its way, unsteady, knock-kneed, towards the udder while the other followed resolutely on its knees.

A lot of the Dales farms were anonymous and it was a help to find this one so plainly identified. 'Heston Grange' it said on the gate in bold black capitals.

I got out of the car and undid the latch. For once it was a good gate, too, and swung easily on its hinges instead of having to be dragged round with a shoulder under the top spar. The farmhouse lay below me, massive, grey-stoned, with a pair of bow windows which some prosperous Victorian had added to the original structure.

It stood on a flat, green neck of land in a loop of the river and the lushness of the grass and the quiet fertility of the surrounding fields contrasted sharply with the stark hills behind. Towering oaks and beeches sheltered the house and a thick pine wood covered the lower slopes of the fell.

I walked round the outbuildings shouting as I always did, because some people considered it a subtle insult to go to the house and ask if the farmer was in. Good farmers are indoors only at meal times. But my shouts drew no reply, so I went over and knocked at the door set deep among the weathered stones.

A voice answered 'Come in', and I opened the door into a huge, stone-flagged kitchen with hams and sides of bacon hanging from hooks in the ceiling. A dark girl in a check blouse and green linen slacks was kneading dough in a bowl. She looked up and smiled. 'Sorry I couldn't let you in. I've got my hands full.' She held up her arms, floury-white to the elbow.

'That's all right. My name is Herriot. I've come to see a calf. It's lame, I understand.'

'Yes, we think he's broken his leg. Probably got his foot in a hole when he was running about. If you don't mind waiting a minute, I'll come with you. My father and the men are in the fields. I'm Helen Alderson, by the way.'

Outside, she turned to me and laughed. 'We've got a bit of a walk, I'm afraid. He's in one of the top buildings. Look, you can just see it up there.' She pointed to a squat, stone barn, high on the fell-side. I knew all about these top buildings; they were scattered all over the high country and I got a lot of healthy exercise going round them. They were used for storing hay and other things and as shelters for the animals on the hill pastures.

I looked at the girl for a few seconds. 'Oh, that's all right, I don't mind. I don't mind in the least.'

We went over the field to a narrow bridge spanning the river. The path led upward through the pine wood and here the sunshine was broken up into islands of brightness among the dark trunks, the sound of the river grew faint and we walked softly on a thick carpet of pine needles. It was cool in the wood and silent except when a bird call echoed through the trees.

Ten minutes of hard walking brought us out again into the hot sun on the open moor and the path curved steeper still round a series of rocky outcrops. I was beginning to puff, but the girl kept up a brisk pace, swinging along with easy strides. I was glad when we reached the the top and the barn came in sight again.

As we left the barn later, the sunshine and the sweet warm air met us like a high wave. I turned and looked across the valley to the soaring green heights, smooth, enormous, hazy in the noon heat. Beneath my feet the grassy slopes fell away steeply to where the river glimmered among the trees.

'It's wonderful up here,' I said. 'Just look at that gorge over there. And that great hill – I suppose you could call it a mountain.' I pointed at a giant which heaved its heather-mottled shoulders high above the others.

'That's Heskit Fell – nearly two and a half thousand feet. And that's Eddleton just beyond, and Wedder Fell on the other side and Colver and Sennor.' The names with their wild, Nordic ring fell easily from her tongue; she spoke of them like old friends and I could sense the affection in her voice.

We sat down on the warm grass of the hillside, a soft breeze pulled at the heads of the moorland flowers, somewhere a curlew cried. Darrowby and Skeldale House and veterinary practice seemed a thousand miles away.

'You're lucky to live here,' I said. 'But I don't think you need me to tell you that.'

'No, I love this country. There's nowhere else quite like it.' She paused and looked slowly around her. 'I'm glad it appeals to you too – a lot of people find it too bare and wild. It almost seems to frighten them.'

I laughed. 'Yes, I know, but as far as I'm concerned I can't help feeling sorry for all the thousands of vets who don't work in the Yorkshire Dales.

If only my car had had any brakes I would certainly have enjoyed looking down on Worton village from the high moor. The old stone houses straggling unevenly along the near bank of the river made a pleasant splash of grey on the green floor of the valley and the little gardens with their clipped lawns gave a touch of softness to the bare, rising sweep of the fellside on the other side of the Dale.

How on earth, did I come to be sitting on a high Yorkshire moor in shirt sleeves and Wellingtons, smelling vaguely of cows? Maybe it was something to do with the incredible sweetness of the air which still took me by surprise when I stepped out into the old wild garden at Skeldale House every morning. Or perhaps the daily piquancy of life in the graceful old house with my gifted but mercurial boss, Siegfried, and his reluctant student brother, Tristan. Or it could be that it was just the realisation that treating cows and pigs and sheep and horses had a fascination I had never even suspected; and this brought with it a new concept of myself as a tiny wheel in the great machine of British agriculture. There was a kind of solid satisfaction in that.

Probably it was because I hadn't dreamed there was a place like the Dales. I hadn't thought it possible that I could spend all my days in a high, clean-blown land where the scent of grass or trees was never far away; and where even in the driving rain of winter I could sniff the air and find the freshness of growing things hidden somewhere in the cold clasp of the wind.

Anyway, it had all changed for me and my work consisted now of driving from farm to farm across the roof of England with a growing conviction that I was a privileged person.

I pulled off the unfenced road on to the grass, switched off the engine and opened the windows wide. The farm back there was like an island of activity in the quiet landscape and now that I was away from the noise and the stuffiness of the buildings the silence and the emptiness enveloped me like a soothing blanket. I leaned my head against the back of the seat and looked out at the chequered greens of the little fields along the flanks of the hills; thrusting upwards between their walls till they gave way to the jutting rocks and the harsh brown of the heather which flooded the wild country above.

I had been away for only two weeks but it was enough to bring it home to me afresh that working in the high country had something for me that was missing elsewhere. My first visit took me up on one of the narrow, unfenced roads which join Sildale and Cosdale and when I had ground my way to the top in bottom gear I did what I so often did – pulled the car on to the roadside turf and got out.

That quotation about not having time to stand and stare has never applied to me. I seem to have spent a good part of my life – probably too much – in just standing and staring and I was at it again this morning. From up here you could see away over the ragged miles of moorland rolling away, dipping and rising over the flat fell-top. In my year at Darrowby I must have stood here scores of times and the view always looked different; sometimes in the winter the low country was a dark trough and in April the rain squalls drifted in slow, heavy veils across the great green and brown dappled expanse. There was a day, too, when I stood in brilliant sunshine looking down into thick fog like a rippling layer of cotton wool with dark tufts of trees and hilltops pushing through here and there.

But today the endless patchwork of fields slumbered in the sun, and the air, even on the hill, was heavy with the scents of summer. There must be people working among the farms down there, I knew, but I couldn't see a living soul; and the peace which I always found in the silence and the emptiness of the moors filled me utterly.

As I drove, I began to catch glimpses over the hedge tops and between the trees of the long spine of the Pennines lifting into the morning sky; they were pale violet at this distance and still hazy in the early sunshine but they beckoned to me. And later, when the little car pulled harder against the rising ground and the trees became fewer and the hedges gave way to the clean limestone walls I had the feeling I always had of the world opening out, of shackles falling away. And there, at last, was Darrowby sleeping under the familiar bulk of Herne Fell and beyond, the great green folds of the Dales.

Nothing stirred as I rattled across the cobbled market place then down the quiet street to Skeldale House with the ivy hanging in untidy profusion from its old bricks and 'Siegfried Farnon, MRCVS' on the lopsided brass plate.

Dennaby Close was not just a substantial farm, it was a monument to a man's endurance and skill. The fine old house, the extensive buildings, the great sweep of lush grass land along the lower slopes of the fell were all proof that old John Skipton had achieved the impossible; he had started as an uneducated farm labourer and he was now a wealthy landowner.

I paused as I got out of the car and stood gazing at the house as though I had never seen it before; and I marvelled again at the elegance which had withstood over three hundred years of the harsh climate. People came a long way to see Dennaby Close and take photographs of the graceful manor with its tall, leaded windows, the massive chimneys towering over the old moss-grown tiles; or to wander through the neglected garden and climb up the sweep of steps to the entrance with its wide stone arch over the great studded door.

Leaving the yard we came on to the quiet loop of road where my car was parked. Just beyond, the road dipped steeply into a tree-lined ravine where the Darrow hurled itself over a great broken shelf of rock in its passage to the lower Dale. I couldn't see down there from where I was standing, but I could hear the faint roar of the water and could picture the black cliff lifting sheer from the boiling river and on the other bank the gentle slope of turf where people from the towns came to sit and look in wonder.

This was the real Yorkshire with the clean limestone wall riding the hill's edge and the path cutting brilliant green through the crowding heather. And, walking face on to the scented breeze I felt the old tingle of wonder at being alone on the wide moorland where nothing stirred and the spreading miles of purple blossom and green turf reached away till it met the hazy blue of the sky.

But I wasn't really alone. There was Sam, and he made all the difference. Helen had brought a lot of things into my life and Sam – a beagle – was one of the most precious. And having him with me added so much to the intermissions I granted myself on my daily rounds. Whereas in offices and factories they had tea breaks I just stopped the car and stepped out into the splendour which was always at hand and walked for a spell down hidden lanes, through woods, or as today, along one of the grassy tracks which ran over the high tops.

This thing which I had always done had a new meaning now. Anybody who has ever walked a dog knows the abiding satisfaction which comes from giving pleasure to a loved animal, and the sight of the little form trotting ahead of me lent a depth which had been missing before.

Round the curve of the path I came to where the tide of heather lapped thickly down the hillside on a little slope facing invitingly into the sun. It was a call I could never resist. I looked at my watch; oh I had a few minutes to spare and there was nothing urgent ahead, just Mr Dacre's tuberculin test. In a moment I was stretched out on the springy stems, the most wonderful natural mattress in the world.

Lying there, eyes half closed against the sun's glare, the heavy heather fragrance around me, I could see the cloud shadows racing across the flanks of the fells, throwing the gulleys and crevices into momentary gloom but trailing a fresh flaring green in their wake.

Those were the days when I was most grateful I was in country practice; the shirt sleeve days when the bleak menace of the bald heights melted into friendliness, when I felt at one with all the airy life and growth about me and was glad that I had become what I never thought I would be, a doctor of farm animals.

I leaned back in my seat and peered through heavy lids at the empty road unwinding in the pale morning light. The sun had just come up – a dark crimson ball hanging low over the misted fields.

The Dixon farm was in the low country where the Dale widened out and gave on to the great Plain of York. I had to cross a loop of the busy road which connected the West Riding with the industrial north-east. A thin tendril of smoke rose from the chimney of the all night transport café which stood there and as I slowed down to take the corner a faint but piercing smell of cooking found its way into the car; the merest breath but rich in the imagery of fried sausages and beans and tomatoes and chips.

This was my second winter in Darrowby so I didn't feel the same sense of shock when it started to be really rough in November. When they were getting a drizzle of rain down there on the plain the high country was covered in a few hours by a white blanket which filled in the roads, smoothed out familiar landmarks, transformed our world into something strange and new. This was what they meant on the radio when they talked about 'snow on high ground'.

When the snow started in earnest it had a strangling effect on the whole district. Traffic crawled laboriously between the mounds thrown up by the snow ploughs. Herne Fell hung over Darrowby like a great gleaming whale and in the town the people dug paths to their gates and cleared the drifts from their front doors. They did it without fuss, with the calm of long use and in the knowledge that they would probably have to do it again tomorrow.

I sat peering delightedly through a flawlessly clear semicircle about eight inches wide at the countryside unwinding before me like a film show; the grey stone villages, silent and withdrawn under their smothering white cloak; the low, burdened branches of the roadside trees.

I was enjoying it so much that I hardly noticed the ache in my toes. Freezing feet were the rule in those days before car heaters, especially when you could see the road flashing past through the holes in the floor boards. On long journeys I really began to suffer towards the end. It was like that today when I got out of the car at the foot of the Pike Edge road; my fingers, too, throbbed painfully as I stamped around and swung my arms.

The ploughs hadn't even attempted to clear the little side road which wound its way upwards and into the valley beyond. Its solid, creamy, wall-to-wall filling said 'No, you can't come up here', with that detached finality I had come to know so ➤

well. But as always, even in my disappointment, I looked with wonder at the shapes the wind had sculpted in the night; flowing folds of the most perfect smoothness tapering to the finest of points, deep hollows with knife-edge rims, soaring cliffs with overhanging margins almost transparent in their delicacy.

Hitching the rucksack on my shoulder I felt a kind of subdued elation. With a leather golf jacket buttoned up to my neck and an extra pair of thick socks under my Wellingtons I felt ready for anything. No doubt I considered there was something just a bit dashing and gallant in the picture of the dedicated young vet with his magic potions on his back battling against the odds to succour a helpless animal.

I stood for a moment gazing at the fell, curving clean and cold into the sullen sky. An expectant hush lay on the fields, the frozen river and the still trees as I took a deap breath started off.

I kept up a good pace. First over a bridge with the river white and silent beneath then up and up, picking my way over the drifts till the road twisted, almost invisible, under some low cliffs. Despite the cold, the sweat was beginning to prick on my back when I got to the top.

I looked around me. I had been up here several times in June and July and I could remember the sunshine, the smell of the warm grass, and the scent of flowers and pines that came up the hill from the valley below. But it was hard to relate the smiling landscape of last summer with this desolation.

The flat moorland on the fell top was a white immensity rolling away to the horizon with the sky pressing down like a dark blanket. I could see the farm down there in its hollow and it, too, looked different; small, remote, like a charcoal drawing against the hills bulking smooth and white beyond. A pine wood made a dark smudge on the slopes but the scene had been wiped clean of most of its familiar features.

I could see the road only in places – the walls were covered over most of their length, but the farm was visible all the way. I had gone about half a mile towards it when a sudden gust of wind blew up the surface snow into a cloud of fine particles. Just for a few seconds I found myself completely alone. The farm, the surrounding moor, everything disappeared and I had an eerie sense of isolation till the veil cleared.

It was hard going in the deep snow and in the drifts I sank over the tops of my Wellingtons. I kept at it, head down, to within a few hundred yards of the stone buildings. I was just thinking that it had all been pretty easy, really, when I looked up and saw a waving curtain of a million black dots bearing down on me. I quickened my steps and just before the blizzard hit me I marked the position of the farm. But after ten minutes' stumbling and slithering I realised I had missed the place. I was heading for a shape that didn't exist; it was etched only in my mind

I stood for a few moments feeling again the chilling sense of isolation. I was convinced I had gone too far to the left and after a few gasping breaths, struck off to the right. It wasn't long before I knew I had gone in the wrong direction again. I began to fall into deep holes, up to the armpits in the snow, reminding me that the ground was not really flat on these high lonely moors but pitted by countless peat hags.

As I struggled on I told myself that the whole thing was ➤

ridiculous. I couldn't be far from the warm fireside at Pike House – this wasn't the North Pole. But my mind went back to the great empty stretch of moor beyond the farm and I had to stifle a feeling of panic.

The numbing cold seemed to erase all sense of time. Soon I had no idea of how long I had been falling into the holes and crawling out. I did know that each time it was getting harder work dragging myself out. And it was becoming more and more tempting to sit down and rest, even sleep; there was something hypnotic in the way the big, soft flakes brushed noiselessly across my skin and mounted thickly on my closed eyes.

I was trying to shut out the conviction that if I fell down many more times I wouldn't get up when a dark shape hovered suddenly ahead. Then my outflung arms touched something hard and rough. Unbelievingly I felt my way over the square stone blocks till I came to a corner. Beyond that was a square of light – it was the kitchen window of the farm.

At the gate I stopped and gazed back at the wide landscape, ribbed and streaked by the last of the winter's snow, and at the dark grey banks of cloud riding across on the wind followed by lakes of brightest blue; and in seconds the fields and walls and woods burst into vivid life and I had to close my eyes against the sun's glare. As I stood there the distant uproar came faintly down to me, the tumultuous harmony from deepest bass to highest treble; demanding, anxious, angry, loving.

The sound of the sheep, the sound of spring.

This was my second spring in the Dales but it was like the one before – and all the springs after. The kind of spring, that is, that a country vet knows; the din of the lambing pens, the bass rumble of the ewes and the high, insistent bawling of the lambs. This, for me, has always heralded the end of winter and the beginning of something new. This and the piercing Yorkshire wind and the hard, bright sunshine flooding the bare hillsides.

Through May and early June my world became softer and warmer. The cold wind dropped and the air, fresh as the sea, carried a faint breath of the thousands of wild flowers which speckled the pastures. At times it seemed unfair that I should be paid for my work; for driving out in the early morning with the fields glittering under the first pale sunshine and the wisps of mist still hanging on the high tops.

At Skeldale House the wistaria exploded into a riot of mauve blooms which thrust themselves through the open windows and each morning as I shaved I breathed in the heady fragrance from the long clusters drooping by the side of the mirror. Life was idyllic.

In the early haze I looked over the countless buttercups; the field was filled with them and it was like sitting in a shimmering yellow ocean. Their pollen had powdered my shoes.

I knew I shouldn't do it, but the old Drovers' Road beckoned to me irresistibly. I ought to be hurrying back to the surgery after my morning call but the broad green path wound beguilingly over the moor top between its crumbling walls and almost before I knew, I was out of the car and treading the wiry grass.

The wall skirted the hill's edge and as I looked across and away to where Darrowby huddled far below between its folding green fells the wind thundered in my ears; but when I squatted in the shelter of the grey stones the wind was only a whisper and the spring sunshine hot on my face. The best kind of sunshine – not heavy or cloying but clear and bright and clean as you find it down behind a wall in Yorkshire with the wind singing over the top.

I slid lower till I was stretched on the turf, gazing with half closed eyes into the bright sky, luxuriating in the sensation of being detached from the world and its problems. This form of self-indulgence had become part of my life and still is; a reluctance to come down from the high country; a penchant for stepping out of the stream of life and loitering on the brink for a few minutes as an uninvolved spectator. And it was easy to escape, lying up here quite alone with no sound but the wind sighing and gusting over the empty miles and, far up in the wide blue, the endless brave trilling of the larks.

In my daily work I was always aware of the beauty around me and had never lost the sense of wonder which had filled me when I had had my first sight of Yorkshire, but this morning the magic of the Dales was stronger than ever.

My eyes strayed again and again over the towering flanks of the fells, taking in the pattern of walled green fields won from the yellow moorland grass, and I gazed up at the high tops with the thrill of excitement which always came down to me from that untrodden land.

After visiting the isolated farm, I couldn't resist pulling my car off the unfenced road and climbing with my beagle to the high country which beckoned me. It was as though all the scents of the earth and growing things had been imprisoned and were released now by the sunshine in waves of a piercing sweetness. When I reached the summit I was breathless and gulped the crystal air greedily as though I could never get enough of it.

Here there was no evidence of the hand of man and I walked with my dog among miles of heather, peat hags and dark bog pools with the black waters rippling and the tufts of rushes bending and swaying in the eternal wind.

As the cloud shadows, racing on the wind, flew over me, trailing ribbons of shade and brightness over the endless browns and greens, I felt a rising exhilaration at just being up there on the roof of Yorkshire. It was an empty landscape where no creature stirred and it was silent except for the cry of a distant bird, yet I felt a further surge of excitement in the solitude, a tingling sense of the nearness of all creation.

It was with a lingering feeling of fulfilment that I finished my last call and headed for Darrowby, the town where I worked. Its square church tower had been pushing above the tumbled roofs of the little town as I came down the dale and soon I was driving through the cobbled market place with the square of fretted roofs above the shops and pubs which served its three thousand inhabitants.

We had to drive ten miles over a desolate moor on the fell top and it was very dark when we rattled down the steep, narrow road into Ellerthorpe. The Wheatsheaf was an unostentatious part of the single long village street, a low grey stone building with no light over the door.

The road to Therby had a few sharp little switchbacks before it dipped down to the village and looking down I could see the long row of silent houses curving away to the base of the fell which by day hung in peaceful green majesty over the huddle of roofs.

I had only to sit up in bed to look right across Darrowby to the hills beyond. I got up and walked to the window. It was going to be a fine morning and the early sun glanced over the weathered reds and greys of the jumbled roofs, some of them sagging under their burden of ancient tiles, and brightened the tufts of green where trees pushed upwards from the gardens among the bristle of chimney pots. And behind everything the calm bulk of the fells.

As I closed the door of Skeldale House and looked along the street to where the first lights of the shops beckoned in the dusk I felt a lifting of the heart. It was as though a breath from the nearby hills had touched me. A fleeting fragrance which said winter had gone. It was still cold – it was always cold in Darrowby until well into May – but the promise was there, of sunshine and warm grass and softer days.

When I left Darrowby the streets of the little town were empty in the gathering dusk and the houses had that tight-shut, comfortable look which raised images of armchairs and pipes and firesides, and now as I saw the lights of the farms winking on the fellsides I could picture the stocksmen dozing contentedly with their feet up.

I had not passed a single car on the darkening road. There was nobody out but Herriot.

Driving away I stopped to open the gate at the end of the track and looked back at the old stone barns crouching against the lower slopes. It was a perfect autumn day with mellow golden sunshine softening the harsh sweep of fell and moor with their striding walls and the air so still and windless that the whirring of a pigeon's wings overhead was loud in the silence. Across the valley on the hilltop a frieze of sparse trees stood as motionless as though they had been painted across the blue canvas of sky.

I drove gingerly down through the wood and before starting up the track on the other side I stopped the car and got out with Sam leaping eagerly after me.

This was a little lost valley in the hills, a green cleft cut off from the wild country above. One of the bonuses in a country vet's life is that he sees these hidden places. Apart from old Arnold nobody ever came down here, not even the postman who left the infrequent mail in a box at the top of the track and nobody saw the blazing scarlets and golds of the autumn trees nor heard the busy clucking and murmuring of the beck among its clean-washed stones.

I walked along the water's edge watching the little fish darting and flitting in the cool depths. In the spring these banks were bright with primroses and in May a great sea of bluebells flowed among the trees but today, though the sky was an untroubled blue, the clean air was touched with the sweetness of the dying year.

I climbed a little way up the hillside and sat down among the bracken now fast turning to bronze. Sam, as was his way, flopped by my side and I ran a hand over the silky hair of his ears. The far side of the valley rose steeply to where, above the gleaming ridge of limestone cliffs, I could just see the sunlit rim of the moor.

Beyond the village the road curved suddenly out of sight of the houses then began the long straight climb to the abbey. Just up there at the limits of my headlights would be where the ghost was always seen – walking across the road and into the black belt of trees. At the top of the hill, on an impulse, I drew in to the side of the road and got out of the car. This was the very place. At the edge of the wood, under the brilliant moon, the smooth boles of the beeches shone with an eerie radiance and, high above, the branches creaked as they swayed in the wind.

I walked into the wood, feeling my way carefully with an arm held before me till I came out on the other side. Raynes Abbey lay before me. I had always associated the beautiful ruin with summer days with the sun warming the old stones of the graceful arches, the chatter of voices, children playing on the cropped turf; but this was 2.30 a.m. in an empty world and the cold breath of the coming winter on my face. I felt suddenly alone.

If I had been able to paint I would have wanted to show how the walls climbed everywhere over the stark fell-sides. I would have tried to capture the magic of the endless empty moors with the reeds trembling over the black bog pools. But Mr Partridge went only for the cosy things; willows hanging by a rustic bridge, village churches, rose-covered cottages.

Outside it was still snowing; city snow drifting down in a wet curtain which soon lost itself in the dirty churned-up slush in the streets. I pulled my coat higher round my neck and huddled deeper in the Bentley's leather luxury.

As if determined to prove his words Granville put his foot down and the great car hurtled along the dead straight stretch of road. We skidded a bit on the corner at Greta Bridge then roared through Bowes and up to the highest country. I could not see much. In fact on the moor top I couldn't see anything, because up there it was the real country snow; big dry flakes driving straight into the headlights and settling comfortably with millions of their neighbours on the already deep white carpet on the road. I just didn't know how Granville was able to see, never mind drive fast; and I had no idea how we were going to get back over here in a few hours' time when the wind had drifted the snow across the road. But I kept my mouth shut. It was becoming increasingly obvious that I emerged as a sort of maiden aunt in Granville's company, so I held my peace and prayed.

We were the only members of the company who were headed eastward and were alone on the road. In fact it occurred to me that we hadn't seen a single car on the road to Appleby and now there was something uncomfortable in our total isolation. The snow had stopped and the brilliant moon flooded its cold light over a white empty world. Empty, that is, except for us, and our solitary state was stressed by the smooth, virgin state of the glistening carpet ahead.

I was conscious of an increasing disquiet as the great gaunt spine of the Pennines bulked before us and as we drew nearer it reared up like an angry white monster.

Past the snow-burdened roofs of Brough then the long climb with the big car slipping from side to side as it fought its way up the bending, twisting hill, engine bellowing. I thought I'd feel better when we reached the top but the first glimpse

of the Bowes Moor road sent my stomach into a lurch of apprehension; miles and miles of it coiling its way across the most desolate stretch of country in all England. And even from this distance you could see the drifts, satin smooth and beautiful, pushing their deadly way across our path.

On either side of the road a vast white desert rolled and dipped endlessly towards the black horizon; there was not a light, not a movement, not a sign of life anywhere.

It happened the next morning by a coincidence that I had a far outlying visit and had to pass the Scotch Corner turning on the North Road. I stopped the car and sat gazing at the long snow-covered road stretching towards the Pennines. I was starting my engine when an AA man came over and spoke at my window.

'You're not thinking of trying the Bowes Moor road, are you?' he said.

'No, no.' I was just looking.

He nodded in satisfaction.

'I'm glad to hear that. It's blocked you know. There hasn't been a car over there for two days.'

Behind him, beyond the open door, the green hillside ran down to the river and the wintry sunshine touched the broad sweep of the shallows with a million dancing lights. A beach of bleached stones gleamed bone-white against the long stretch of grassy bank which rolled up to the pastures lining the valley floor.

I had often felt that this smallholding would be an ideal place to live; only a mile outside Darrowby, but secluded, and with this heart-lifting vista of river and fell. I remarked on this once to Mr Dakin and the old man turned to me with a wry smile.

'Aye, but the view's not very sustainin'; he said.

We used to have fogs in Darrowby, but they were country fogs, different from this. One morning I drove out on my rounds with the headlights blazing against the grey curtain ahead, seeing nothing from my tight-shut box. But I was heading up the Dale, climbing steadily with the engine pulling against the rising ground, then quite suddenly the fog thinned to a shimmering silvery mist and was gone. And there, above the pall, the sun was dazzling and the long green line of the fells rose before me, thrusting exultantly into a sky of summer blue.

Spellbound, I drove upwards into the bright splendour, staring through the windscreen as though I had never seen it all before; the brown of the old bracken spilling down the grassy flanks of the hills, the dark smudges of trees, the grey farmhouses and the endless pattern of walls creeping to the heather above.

I was in a rush as usual but I had to stop. I pulled up in a gateway, Sam jumped out and we went through into a field; and as the beagle scampered over the glittering turf I stood in the warm sunshine amid the melting frost and looked back at the dark damp blanket which blotted out the low country but left this jewelled world above it.

And, gulping the sweet air, I gazed about me gratefully at the clean green land where I worked and made my living. I could have stayed there, wandering round, watching Sam exploring with waving tail, nosing into the shady corners where the sun had not reached and the ground was iron hard and the rime thick and crisp on the grass. But I had an appointment to keep.

The next call was to a sick pig, high on Marstang Fell. The road took me at first along the fertile valley floor, winding under the riverside trees past substantial farmhouses and rich pastures; but as the car left the road and headed up a steep track the country began to change. The transition was almost violent as the trees and bushes thinned out and gave way to the bare, rocky hillside and the miles of limestone walls. And though the valley had been rich with the fresh green of the new leaves, up here the buds were unopened and the naked branches stretched against the sky still had the look of winter.

Tim Alton's farm lay at the top of the track and as I pulled up at the gate I wondered as I always did how the man could scrape a living from those few harsh acres with the grass flattened and yellowed by the wind which always blew. At any rate, many generations had accomplished the miracle and had lived and struggled and died in that house with its outbuildings crouching in the lee of a group of stunted, wind-bent trees, its massive stones crumbling under three centuries of fierce wild weathering.

Why should anybody want to build a farm in such a place? I turned as I opened the gate, and looked back at the track threading between the walls down and down to where the white stones of the river glittered in the spring sunshine. Maybe the builder had stood here, and looked across the green vastness and breathed in the cold, sweet air and thought it was enough.

It was mid morning when we rumbled into the market place and I read 'Darrowby Co-operative Society' above the shop on the far side. The sun was high, warming the tiles of the fretted line of roofs with their swelling green background of hills. I got out and the bus went on its way, leaving me standing by my case.

And it was just the same as before. The sweet air, the silence and the cobbled square deserted except for the old men sitting around the clock tower. One of them looked up at me.

'Now then, Mr Herriot,' he said quietly as though he had seen me only yesterday.

Before me Trengate curved away till it disappeared round the grocer's shop on the corner. Most of the quiet street with the church at its foot was beyond my view and it was a long time since I had been down there, but with my eyes closed I could see Skeldale House with the ivy climbing over the old brick walls to the little rooms under the eaves.

III

Hedwick was at the top end of Allerdale, a smaller offshoot of the main Dale, and as we drove up the deep ever-narrowing cleft in the moorland I wound down the window. It was the sort of country I saw every day but I wasn't used to being a passenger and there was no doubt you could see more this way. From the overlapping fringe of heather far above, the walls ran in spidery lines down the bare green flanks to the softness of the valley floor where grey farmhouses crouched; and the heavy scent of the new cut hay lying in golden swathes in the meadows drifted deliciously into the car. There were trees, too, down here, not the stunted dwarfs of the high country above us, but giants in the exultant foliage of high summer.

We stopped at Hedwick because we could go no further. This was the head of the Dale, a cluster of cottages, a farm and a pub.

I followed the usual route down to the river where the water ran dark and silent under the branches of the gnarled willows. Then we went over the bridge and in front of us the river widened into pebbly shallows and murmured and chattered among the stones. It was peaceful down there with only the endless water sound and the piping of birds in my ears and the long curtain of leaves parting here and there to give glimpses of the green flanks of the fells.

There is plenty of time for thinking during the long hours of driving. From the warm darkness the grass smell of the Dales stole through the open window and as I drove through a silent village it was mingled briefly with the mysterious sweetness of wood smoke. Beyond the houses the road curved smooth and empty between the black enclosing fells.

Ted's smallholding was a grey smudge high on a hillside near the top of the dale. There was no road to it and my car bumped its way up the grassy slope with my drugs and instruments rattling and clinking behind me. The flagged yard and thick-walled buildings were hundreds of years old; in fact, coupled with its inaccessibility, it was the sort of place where only hard-up people like Ted would dream of trying to make a living.

I packed up my gear and we went outside. Breathing in the cold, clean air I looked at the cloud shadows chasing across the tumbled miles of green hills, and at the few acres that were Ted's world. They made a little wall-girt island lapped around by the tufted grass of the moorland which was always trying to flow over and swamp it. Those fields had to be fed and fertilised to keep them from returning to their wild state, and the walls, twisted and bent by the centuries, kept shedding their stones — another job to be done by that one man. I recalled a time when Ted told me that one of his luxuries was to wake up in the middle of the night so that he could turn over and go to sleep again.

As I started the engine, he waved, raising a huge, work-calloused hand. Bumping down the hillside I looked back at the thin, slightly stooping figure standing by the house with its fringe of stunted trees, and an awareness of his situation welled in me as it had done so often before. Compared to his, my life was a picnic.

I did what I usually did when I was worried; drove off the unfenced road, got out of the car and followed a track across the moor. The track wound beneath the brow of the fell which overlooked the Mount farm and when I had left the road far behind I flopped on the grass and looked down on the sunlit valley floor a thousand feet below.

In most places you could hear something – the call of a bird, a car in the distance – but here there was a silence which was absolute, except when the wind sighed over the hill top, rustling the bracken around me. The farm lay in one of the soft places on a harsh countryside; lush flat fields where cattle grazed in comfort and the cut hay lay in long even swathes.

It was a placid scene, but it was up here in the airy heights that you found true serenity. Peace dwelt here in the high moorland, stealing across the empty miles, breathing from the silence and the tufted grass and the black, peaty earth.

The heady fragrance of the hay rose in the warm summer air and as always I felt my troubles dissolving. Even now, after all the years, I still count myself lucky that I can so often find tranquillity of mind in the high places.

As I rose to go I was filled with a calm resolve. I would do the job somehow. Surely I could manage the thing without troubling Siegfried.

Sitting on the bus, still with my cap on my lap to avoid attracting attention, it struck me that the whole world changed within a mile or two as we left the town. Back there the war was everywhere, filling people's minds and thoughts; the teeming thousands of uniformed men, the RAF and army vehicles, the almost palpable atmosphere of anticipation and suspense. And suddenly it all just stopped.

It vanished as the wide sweep of grey-blue sea fell beneath the rising ground behind the town, and as the bus trundled westward I looked out on a landscape of untroubled peace. The long moist furrows of the new-turned soil glittered under the pale autumn sun, contrasting with the gold stubble fields and the grassy pastures where sheep clustered around their feeding troughs. There was no wind and the smoke rose straight from the farm chimneys and the bare branches of the roadside trees were still as they stretched across the cold sky.

There were many things that pulled at me. An old man in breeches and leggings carrying on his shoulder a bale of hay to some out-lying cattle; a group of farm men burning hedge clippings and the fragrance of the wood smoke finding its way into the bus. The pull was stronger as the hours passed and the beginnings of my own familiar countryside began to appear beyond the windows.

Mind you, it was cold. Yorkshire is a cold place and I could remember the sensation almost of shock at the start of my first winter in Darrowby.

It was after the first snow and I followed the clanging ploughs up the Dale, bumping along between high white mounds till I reached old Mr Stokill's gate. With my fingers on the handle I looked through the glass at the new world beneath me. The white blanket rolled down the hillside and lapped over the roofs of the dwelling and outbuildings of the little farm. Beyond, it smoothed out and concealed the familiar features, the stone walls bordering the fields, the stream on the valley floor, turning the whole scene into something unknown and exciting.

But the thrill I felt at the strange beauty was swept away as I got out and the wind struck me. It was an Arctic blast screaming from the east, picking up extra degrees of cold as it drove over the frozen white surface. I was wearing a heavy overcoat and woollen gloves but the gust whipped its way right into my bones. I gasped and leaned my back against the car while I buttoned the coat up under my chin, then I struggled forward to where the gate shook and rattled. I fought it open and my feet crunched as I went through.

As I drove away the darkness was thinning into the grey beginning of a new day and around me the white bulk of the fells began to lift from the half light – massive, smooth and inexpressibly cold.

There are all kinds of barns. Some of them are small, cosy and fragrant with hay, but this was a terrible place. I had been in here on sunny afternoons and even then the dank gloom of crumbling walls and rotting beams was like a clammy blanket and all warmth and softness seemed to disappear among the cobwebbed rafters high above. I used to feel that people with starry eyed notions of farming ought to take a look inside that barn. It was evocative of the grim comfortless other side of the agricultural life.

I had it to myself now, and as I stood there listening to the wind rattling the door on its latch a variety of draughts whistled round me and a remorseless drip-drip from the broken pantiles on the roof sent icy droplets trickling over my head and neck. And as the minutes ticked away I began to hop from foot to foot in a vain effort to keep warm.

Long Pasture Farm was in the little hamlet of Dowsett and I had travelled this narrow road many times. It snaked its way high into the wild country and on summer days the bare lonely hills had a serene beauty; treeless and austere, but with a clean wind sweeping over the grassy miles.

It was a large field and I could see the barn at the far end as I walked with the tall grass brushing my knees. It was a meadow ready for cutting and suddenly I realised that it was high summer, the sun was hot and that every step brought the fragrance of clover and warm grass rising about me into the crystal freshness of the air. Somewhere nearby a field of broad beans was in full flower and as the exotic scent drifted across I found myself inhaling with half-closed eyes as though straining to discern the ingredients of the glorious mélange.

And then there was the silence; it was the most soothing thing of all. That and the feeling of being alone. I looked drowsily around at the empty green miles sleeping under the late afternoon sunshine. Nothing stirred, there was no sound.

I was almost drowning in self-pity when I turned into the tiny village of Copton. In the warm days of summer it was idyllic, reminding me always of a corner of Perthshire, with its single street hugging the lower slopes of a green hillside and a dark drift of trees spreading to the heathery uplands high above.

But tonight it was a dead black place with the rain sweeping across the headlights against the tight-shut houses; except for a faint glow right in the middle where the light from the village pub fell softly on the streaming roadway. I stopped the car under the swinging sign of the Fox and Hounds and on an impulse opened the door. A beer would do me good.

I was on the way to Len's farm and on an impulse I pulled up the car and leaned for a moment on the wheel. It was a hot still day in late summer and this was one of the softer corners of the Dales, sheltered by the enclosing fells from the harsh winds which shrivelled all but the heather and the tough moorland grass.

Here, great trees, oak, elm and sycamore in full rich leaf, stood in gentle majesty in the green dips and hollows, their branches quite still in the windless air. In all the grassy miles around me I could see no movement, nor could I hear anything except the fleeting hum of a bee and the distant bleating of a sheep.

Through the open window drifted the scents of summer; warm grass, clover and the sweetness of hidden flowers. But in the car they had to compete with the all-pervading smell of cow. I had spent the last hour injecting fifty wild cattle and I sat there in soiled breeches and sweat-soaked shirt looking out sleepily at the tranquil landscape.

I opened the door and Sam jumped out and trotted into a nearby wood. I followed him into the cool shade, into the damp secret fragrance of pine needles and fallen leaves which came from the dark heart of the crowding boles. From somewhere in the branches high above I could hear that most soothing of sounds, the cooing of a woodpigeon.

It was about a month later, on a market day, and I was strolling among the stalls which packed the cobbles. In front of the entrance to the Drovers' Arms the usual press of farmers stood chatting among themselves, talking business with cattle dealers and corn merchants, while the shouts of the stallholders sounded over everything.

The situation of East Farm seemed to add weight to my words. We were bumping up the fellside along a narrow track which was never meant for motor cars and I winced as the exhaust grated against the jutting rocks. The farm was perched almost on the edge of the hilltop and behind it the sparse fields, stolen from the moorland, rolled away to the skyline. The crumbling stonework and broken roof tiles testified to the age of the squat grey house.

141

It's lovely weather,' Helen said, slipping her arm through mine. 'Let's have a picnic tomorrow.'

One thing about living in Darrowby is that you don't have to drive very far to leave the town behind. Next day we sat down on a grassy bank and as we opened our packet of sandwiches the September sun flooded down, warming the grey stones of the wall behind us, slanting dazzlingly against the tumbling water of the river far below. Beyond the wall lay the wide golden sweep of a corn field and a little breeze stirred the ripe ears into a long slow whisper, bringing with it the sweet scent of a thousand growing things.

Animals are the same as people. They need friends. Have you ever watched two animals in a field? They may be of different species – a pony and a sheep – but they hang together. This comradeship between animals has always fascinated me.

At last we were on our way to Flying School. It was at Windsor and that didn't seem far on the map, but it was a typical wartime journey of endless stops and changes and interminable waits. It went on all through the night and we took our sleep in snatches. I stole an hour's fitful slumber on the waiting-room table at a tiny nameless station and despite my hard pillowless bed I drifted deliciously back to Darrowby.

I was bumping along the rutted track to Nether Lees Farm, hanging on to the jerking wheel. I could see the house below me, its faded red tiles showing above the sheltering trees, and behind the buildings the scrubby hillside rose to the moor.

Up there the trees were stunted and sparse and dotted widely over the steep flanks. Higher still there was only scree and cliff and right at the top, beckoning in the sunshine, I saw the beginning of the moor – smooth, unbroken and bare.

A scar on the broad sweep of green showed where long ago they quarried the stones to build the massive farmhouses and the enduring walls which have stood against the unrelenting climate for hundreds of years. Those houses and those end-lessly marching walls would still be there when I was gone and forgotten.

Helen was with me in the car. I loved it when she came with me on my rounds, and after the visit to the farm we climbed up the fellside, panting through the scent of the warm bracken, feeling the old excitement as we neared the summit.

Then we were on the top, facing into the wide free moorland and the clean Yorkshire wind and the cloud shadows racing over the greens and browns. Helen's hand was warm in mine as we wandered among the heather through green islets nibbled to a velvet sward by the sheep. She raised a finger as a curlew's lonely cry sounded across the wild tapestry and the wonder in her eyes shone through the dark flurry of hair blowing across her face.

The gentle shaking at my shoulder pulled me back to wakefulness, to the hiss of steam and the clatter of boots. The table top was hard against my hip and my neck was stiff where it had rested on my pack.

'Train's in, Jim.' An airman was looking down at me. 'I hated to wake you – you were smiling.'

I increased my speed as I drove through Darrowby. The cobbled market place, sleeping in the sunshine, breathed its Sunday peace and emptiness with all the inhabitants of the little town eating busily behind closed doors.

It was always something of a safari to visit Anson Hall, because the old house lay at the end of a ridged and rutted track which twisted across the fields through no fewer than seven gates. Gates are one of the curses of a country vet's life and in the Yorkshire Dales, before the coming of cattle grids, we suffered more than most. We were resigned to opening two or three on many of the farms, but seven was a bit much.

One still summer evening I was returning from a call when I stopped the car and wound down the window. The fells rose around me, their summits glinting in the last sunshine, but the only living creatures were the cattle and sheep grazing on the slopes.

Alone in the cold darkness I looked at the gaunt silhouette of the old farmhouse above me. In the dying light of the November day the rain streamed down the rough stones and the wind caught at the thin tendril of smoke from the chimney, hurling it in ragged streamers across the slate blue pallor of the western sky. The fell hung over everything, a black featureless bulk, oppressive and menacing.

Through the kitchen window I could see the oil lamp casting its dim light over the bare table, the cheerless hearth with its tiny flicker of fire. In the shadows at the far end the steps rose into Ned's loft and I could imagine the little figure clambering up to get changed and escape to Briston.

Across the valley the single street of the village was a broken grey thread in the gloom but in the cottage windows the lamps winked faintly. These were Ned Finch's bright lights and I could understand how he felt. After Scar Farm, Briston would be like Monte Carlo.

With my hand on the car door I looked back at Scar Farm, at the sagging roof tiles, the great stone lintel over the door. It typified the harshness of the lives of the people within. Ned was no bargain as a stocksman, and his boss's exasperation was understandable. Mr Daggett was not a cruel or an unjust man. He and his wife had been hardened and squeezed dry by the pitiless austerity of their existence in this lonely corner of the high Pennines.

There was no softness up here, no frills. The stone walls, sparse grass and bent stunted trees; the narrow road with its smears of cow muck. Everything was down to fundamentals, and it was a miracle to me that most of the Dalesmen were not like the Daggetts but cheerful and humorous.

But as I drove away, the sombre beauty of the place overwhelmed me. The lowering hillsides burst magically into life as a shaft of sunshine stabbed through the clouds, flooding the bare flanks with warm gold. Suddenly I was aware of the delicate shadings of green, the rich glowing bronze of the dead bracken spilling from the high tops, the whole peaceful majesty of my work-a-day world.

The high moorland road was unfenced and my car wheels ran easily from the strip of tarmac on to the turf cropped to a velvet closeness by the sheep. I stopped the engine, got out and looked around me.

The road cut cleanly through the grass and heather before dipping into the valley beyond. This was one of the good places where I could see into two dales, the one I had left and the one in front. The whole land was spread beneath me; the soft fields in the valley floors, the grazing sheep, and the rivers, pebbled at their edges in places, thickly fringed with trees at others.

The brilliant green of the walled pastures pushed up the sides of the fells until the heather and the harsh moor grass began, and only the endless pattern of walls was left climbing to the mottled summits, disappearing over the bare ridges which marked the beginning of the wild country.

I leaned back against the car and the wind blew the cold sweet air around me. I had been only a few weeks back in civilian life, and during my time in RAF blue I had thought constantly of Yorkshire, but I had forgotten how beautiful it was. Just thinking from afar could not evoke the peace, the solitude, the sense of the nearness of the wild which makes the Dales thrilling and comforting at the same time. Among the crowds of men and the drabness and stale air of the towns I could not really imagine a place where I could be quite alone on the wide green roof of England, and where every breath was filled with the grass scent.

It was the year of the great snow, 1947. I have never known snow like that before or since and the odd thing was that it took such a long time to get started. Nothing happened in November and we had a green Christmas, but then it began to get colder and colder. All through January a north-east wind blew, apparently straight from the Arctic, and usually after a few days of this sort of unbearable blast, snow would come and make things a bit warmer. But not in 1947.

Each day we thought it couldn't get any colder, but it did, and then, borne on the wind, very fine flakes began to appear over the last few days of the month. They were so small you could hardly see them but they were the forerunners of the real thing. At the beginning of February big, fat flakes started a steady relentless descent on our countryside and we knew, after all that build-up, that we were for it.

For weeks and weeks the snow fell, sometimes in a gentle, almost lazy curtain which remorselessly obliterated the familiar landmarks, at others in fierce blizzards. In between, the frost took over and transformed the roads into glassy tracks of flattened snow over which we drove at fifteen miles an hour.

It had been bitterly cold all day and the wind had that piercing quality which usually precedes snow. I wasn't surprised when, around eight o'clock that evening, the big white flakes began to drift down and within an hour the countryside was blanketed in white. The snow stopped then and I was grateful, because a heavy fall made it almost impossible to reach some of the high farms. A shovel was essential equipment.

When I had a call at seven o'clock next morning to a calving at a remote smallholding at the top of the dale, I was relieved that no more snow had fallen during the night. I had finished the job by nine o'clock and as I drove home, warm with the satisfaction which the delivery of a live calf always gives me, I marvelled at the new world around me. It was always beautiful up there, but the snow had made a magical change, adding a white stillness and peace.

I was looking at the delicate roadside drifts which the wind had shaped so exquisitely in the night when I saw the gate to Mr Whitehead's farm. It was a good chance to check on those calves and I turned my car along the lane.

It was a long, long road, not much more than a rough track, trailing ever upwards for nearly a mile, disappearing from time to time behind bluffs or rocky outcrops until it reached the farm whose faded red roofs were just visible as I drove up to the first gate.

These farms of many gates were places of dread on busy days, eating up the precious minutes with nothing to show for all the effort. But this particular morning, as I got out of the car, the sun struck warm on my face and the crisp air tingled in my nostrils and, pushing back gate one, I looked around at the wide landscape, silent and peaceful under its white mantle, and blessed my good fortune. There were six of these gates, and I hopped out happily at each one, the snow crackling under my feet.

Five o'clock in the morning and the telephone jangling in my ear. Ewe lambing at Walton's, a lonely farm on the high moorland, and as I crawled from the haven of bed into the icy air of the bedroom and began to pull on my clothes, I tried not to think of the comfortless hour or two ahead.

Through the tight-shut, sleeping little town, then on to the narrow road winding between its walls until the trees dwindled and disappeared, leaving the wide windswept fells bare and unwelcoming at this hour.

I wondered if there was any chance of the ewe being under cover. In the early fifties, it didn't seem to occur to many of the farmers to bring their lambing ewes into the buildings and I attended to the great majority out in the open fields. There were happy times when I almost chuckled in relief at the sight of a row of hurdles in a warm fold yard or sometimes the farmers would build pens from stacked-up straw bales, but on this occasion my spirits plummeted when I drew up at the farm and met Mr Walton who came out of the house carrying a bucket of water and headed for the gate.

'Outside, is she?' I asked, trying to sound airy.

'Aye, just ower there.' He pointed over the long, bracken-splashed pasture to a prone woolly form in the distance which looked a hell of a long way 'ower there'. As I trailed across the frosty grass, my medical bag and obstetric overall dangling, a merciless wind tore at me, picking up an extra Siberian cold from the long drifts of snow which still lay behind the walls in this late Yorkshire spring.

As I stripped off and knelt behind the ewe I looked around. We were right on top of the world and the panorama of hills and valleys with grey farmhouses and pebbled rivers in their depths was beautiful but would have been more inviting if it had been a warm summer afternoon and me preparing for a picnic with my family.

I drove away from the farm and pulled up the car in the lee of a dry-stone wall. I leaned back against the seat and closed my eyes.

When I opened them a few minutes later, the sun had broken through the clouds, bringing the green hillsides and the sparkling ridges of snow to vivid life, painting the rocky outcrops with gold. I wound down the window and breathed in the cold clean air drifting down, fresh and tangy, from the moorland high above. A curlew cried, breaking the enveloping silence, and on the grassy bank by the roadside I saw the first primroses of spring.

It was good to be able to work with animals in this thrilling countryside; I was lucky to be a vet in the Yorkshire Dales.

Calum gave me a friendly dig in the ribs. 'I wish you'd come with me to watch the deer one morning, Jim. I keep asking you, but I can never pin you down.'

I didn't know what to say. Part of me wanted a glimpse of Calum's world of nature – he spent all his spare time roaming the countryside, studying the plants and flowers, observing the habits of the wild creatures – but I felt woefully ignorant by comparison. I had grown up in the big city of Glasgow and though I had fallen in love with the Yorkshire countryside I knew that a deep knowledge of flora and fauna was something best acquired in childhood. Siegfried had it, both my children had it and were always trying to educate me, but I knew I'd never be an expert. Certainly not like Calum. He was steeped in the things of the wild. It was his consuming passion.

'Tomorrow, eh?' As the level of my glass went down, my doubts began to evaporate. 'Well maybe I could make it.'

'Great, great.' My colleague ordered two more pints. 'We'll go up to Steadforth Woods. I've built a hide there.'

'Steadforth Woods? Surely there aren't any deer in there.'

Calum gave me a secret smile. 'Oh yes, there are – lots of them.'

'Well, I'm amazed. I've passed those woods a thousand times. I've walked my dogs through them, but I've never seen a trace of a deer.'

'You'll see some tomorrow. Just you wait.'

'Okay. When do we start?'

He rubbed his hands. 'I'll pick you up at three o'clock.'

'*Three o'clock!* As early as that?'

'Oh yes, we've got to be there before daybreak.'

As I finished my second pint the whole thing seemed pleasantly attractive. Up and away before the dawn to plumb the secrets of the woods. I could not understand my previous misgivings.

I felt different the next morning when the alarm blasted in my ear at 2.45 am. Years of being jerked from slumber in the small hours had bred in me a fierce love of my bed, and here I was deliberately quitting the warm nest to drive out into the cold darkness and sit in a wood – just for fun. I must be mad.

When I met Calum, it was clear he didn't share my feelings. He was bubbling with enthusiasm and he laughed as he thumped me on the shoulder. 'You're going to love this, Jim. I've really been looking forward to doing this with you.'

I shivered as I got into his car. It was bitterly cold and the street was like a pitch black well. I huddled in the seat and Calum drove away whistling. He kept up a bright chatter on the way and it was easy to see that this was Calum in his natural element, roaming the countryside while the world was asleep.

We climbed a fence and he led me for a long way among the dark trunks into the very heart of the wood, to his hide which he had built near a clearing. In the first pale light I could see that it was a well-hidden place, carefully constructed of branches of larch and spruce and tufts of grass.

'Sit here,' whispered my colleague. He was clearly in a state of high excitement, his eyes wide, a half smile on his face. ➤

We hadn't long to wait. As the dawn light filtered through the branches, there was a rustling and a sound of movement among the trees, then, one by one, the deer began to appear in the clearing. Through all the years I had never seen a deer in these woods but here they were there in profusion; gentle does and majestic, antlered stags moving around, cropping the grass. It was a scene of indescribable peace and beauty, and with the feeling that I was a privileged observer I sat there enthralled. There was a badger sett nearby and Calum pointed in delight as his favourite animals came out to play with their young.

Afterwards we walked through the scented silence of the woods, the pine needles soft under our feet, and he talked, not only about the deer, but about the other wild creatures of the forest and about the plants and flowers which flourished in those secret places. He seemed to know it all and I began to understand the depths of the interest which coloured his entire life. He held the key to a magic world.

As we reached the field the sun came out and, looking back, I could see long drifts of bluebells among the dark boles of the trees, and in the glades, where the first rays struck through the branches, primroses and anemones shone like scattered jewels.

When I returned to the surgery there was one visit waiting for me, high in the hills, and the journey up there was like a happy dream. It seemed that all nature was rejoicing with me. It was the ninth of May, 1947, the beginning of the most perfect summer I can remember. The sun blazed, soft breezes swirled into the car, carrying their fragrance from the fells around, an elusive breath of the bluebells, primroses and violets scattered everywhere on the grass and flowing among the shadows of the trees.

After I had seen my patient, I took a walk along a favourite path with Sam trotting at my heels. I looked away over the rolling patchwork of the fields sleeping in the sun's haze and at the young bracken on the hillside springing straight and green from last year's dead brown stalks. Everywhere new life was calling out its exultant message, and it was so apt with my new little daughter not far away in Darrowby.

On that May day I caught myself just in time. It has always been my practice to recline in the sunshine on the springy bed of heather which clusters on these hillsides and I was just settling down when I remembered I had other things to do today. I sped back to Skeldale House and began to telephone my glad news all over the country.

The Boynton smithy stood right at the end of Rolford village and as I drove up to the squat building with its clustering trees and backdrop of green hillside I felt, as I often did, that I was looking at one of the last relics of the past. When I first came to Yorkshire, every village had its blacksmith's shop and Darrowby itself had several. But with the disappearance of the draught horse they had just melted away. The men who had spent their lives in them for generations had gone and their work places which had echoed to the clatter of horses' feet and the clang of iron were deserted and silent.

Any notion we might have harboured of celebrating an exciting wedding was soon quashed, and in a way which I realised was typical of them. They slipped away quietly to Keeler church and the ceremony was carried out there without fuss.

I have never in my travels through Britain seen anything quite like Keeler. It is an ancient church of great beauty built by the Normans around 1100, standing quite alone among surrounding fields. There is a farm nearby but the nearest village is two miles away. It is on the borders of our practice area, but it can be clearly seen from the main road and whenever I drive past I always slow down to look yet again at that lovely building, solitary among the fields with the hills rising behind. To me, it is a romantic, thrilling sight.

Throughout the centuries, services have been conducted regularly there with a small congregation drawn from the surrounding farms and nearby villages, so that the church has been preserved in all its glory. Its beauty is a stark beauty of massive stone with nothing like the traceried battlements and buttresses of Darrowby's splendid church which is famed to such an extent that it is sometimes referred to as a little cathedral. Helen and I were married there and have never ceased to be enthralled by its sheer magnificence.

However, Calum and Deirdre went to Keeler in its wild and lonely setting and I could understand its appeal which would reach out to them. There was a brief honeymoon and that was all.

Whenever I pass the old church standing in its solitary dignity looking over the empty fields and the long line of hills as it has done for nine centuries, I think again how fitting it was that those young Buchanans should pledge their future life within its walls.

Afterwards, in the May sunshine, Helen and I climbed with our dog behind the house, up the grassy bank, past trees heavy with blossom, then over a stile to a lofty green plateau which seemed to overlook the whole world.

We flopped on to the grass and from our eyrie we looked down past the sheep unhurriedly cropping the grass to the house lying below us. Behind us was a great crescent of tree-covered hillside with the rim of the high moorland peeping above the trees. This majestic sweep curved away to a headland where a tall cliff dominated the scene – a huge friendly slab of rock gleaming in the sunshine. Away in the other direction, over the roofs of the hamlet, there was a heart-lifting glimpse of the great wide Plain of York and the distant hills beyond.

After a cold spring, the whole countryside had softened and the air had a gentle warmth, rich with the scents of May blossom and the medley of wild flowers which speckled the grass. In a little wood to our right a scented lake of bluebells flooded the shady reaches of the trees.

As we sat there, three squirrels hopped one after another from a tall sycamore and, pursued optimistically by the dog, flitted, quick and light as air, over the greensward and disappeared behind a rise, leaving her effortlessly behind.

Helen voiced my thoughts. 'Living here would be heaven.'

We almost ran down the hill to the house and closed the deal with the doctor. There were none of the traumas of our previous house-buying efforts; a shake of the hand and it was over.

Helen's words were prophetic. It was a sad moment when we had to leave the happy memories of Rowan Garth behind, but once we were installed in High Field we realised that living in Hannerly was heaven indeed. At times I could hardly believe our luck. To be able to sit outside our front door, drinking tea in the sunshine and watching the mallard splashing and diving on our pond; with the hillside before us aflame with gorse and, away above, that changeless cliff face smiling down. And to live always in a quiet world where the silence at night was almost palpable.

Picking my torchlit way with the dog on our nocturnal strolls I could hear nothing except the faintest whisper of the beck murmuring its eternal way under the stone bridge. Sometimes on these nightly walks, a badger would scuttle across my path, and under the stars I might see a fox carrying out a stealthy exploration of our lawn.

One morning on an early call just after dawn, I surprised two roe deer in the open and watched enthralled as they galloped at incredible speed across the fields and, clearing the fences like steeplechasers, plunged into the woods.

Here in Hannerly, just a few miles from Darrowby, there was the ever present thrill for Helen and me that we were now living on the edge of the wild.

It was a golden afternoon in late October and beyond the stone walls the fellsides, ablaze with their mantle of dead bracken, rose serenely into a deep, unbroken blue. We passed under a long canopy of tinted leaves thrown over us by the roadside trees then followed a stretch of white-pebbled river before turning along a narrow track which led up the hillside.

Andrew was silent as we climbed into the stark, airy solitude which is the soul of the Dales, but as the track levelled out on the summit he put a hand on my arm.

'Just stop a minute, Jim, will you?' he said.

I pulled up and wound down the window. For a few moments he looked out over the miles of heathery moorland and the rounded summits of the great hills slumbering in the sunshine, then he spoke quietly as though to himself.

'So this is where you work?'

'Yes, this is it, Andy.'

He took a long breath, then another as if greedy for more.

'You know,' he said. 'I've heard a lot about air like wine, but this is the first time I've realised what it means.'

I nodded. I always felt I could never get enough of that air; sharp and cool and tinged only with the grass scent which lingers in the high country.

The extracts in this book have been taken from the eight books of the James Herriot stories which are all © The James Herriot Partnership

For those readers who would like to know the area in which the majority of photographs were taken will find the following information helpful, but it should be stressed that they are very rarely the places described by the author in the text extract facing the photograph. As is mentioned in Jim Wight's introduction, very few people other than his father knew exactly the places he was describing and, more often than not, they were an amalgam of several places.